STUDIO DB

# DRAWN
# TOGETHER
## STUDIO DB

ARCHITECTURE AND INTERIORS

**Britt and Damian Zunino**
with Tim McKeough

Foreword by Chai Vasarhelyi and Jimmy Chin
Principal photography by Matthew Williams

New York · Paris · London · Milan

CONTENTS

# FOREWORD

Chai Vasarhelyi and Jimmy Chin

As filmmakers, we love to tell stories. When we're looking for new subjects, we always ask questions. What is the story here? How is this story different from one we've told before? Why are we telling it?

When we were planning our New York City apartment, we asked similar questions. We wanted every room to tell a story. We wanted each detail to have meaning for our family, as well as a sense of humor. We wanted to be reminded, whether we're coming home from a busy day in the city or a monthslong expedition, that we can still be who we are without taking ourselves too seriously. We wanted to create rooms that would bring smiles to visitors' faces and contribute a small moment of joy to each day.

But we make movies; we don't design rooms. That's where Studio DB came in. We connected instantly with Britt and Damian because they viewed our home as an opportunity to tell our family story through design. The custom terrazzo floor in the entry gallery incorporates stones from our adventures in Jackson. The de Gournay wallpaper in the dining room was created using traditional chinoiserie techniques that respect both our Chinese heritage and our love of the mountains. And when we thought to personalize the wallpaper, they helped us add an unexpected pop of color in the neon-pink blossoms on the trees. They truly created a home that reflects us and our stories.

When it came time to build a new office for our company, Little Monster Films, we trusted Studio DB again. They already had an understanding of our aesthetic and how the two of us move through the world. This time, they created a space that met all our professional needs but included touches of whimsy that express so much about us and our company. The screening room is highly technical, but includes vintage Carlo Scarpa chairs they covered in colorful, playful fabric, in addition to traditional velvet. Their work is thoughtful and considerate, but they are never afraid to do something unexpected and exciting.

The personal and professional dynamic between Britt and Damian is very similar to our own. As husband and wife, parents, business partners, and creative professionals, we understand the challenges that come with living every part of our lives together. Like us, they approach projects from very different viewpoints and then work to bring their respective ideas together. As we know well, this is rarely a seamless process, but their work benefits from that tension. We all end up finding a deeper and more mean-ingful expression in our craft because of these dynamics. That dialogue is something that's extremely rewarding to have with your partner.

We have loved working with Britt, Damian, and their amazing team and are honored to be included in this wonderful book.

# INTRODUCTION

We're not just interested in design. We live and breathe design. It is central to our lives and has carried us to places we would have never experienced otherwise. We probably wouldn't even have met if it weren't for design. Our first encounter happened to lead directly to our first project together.

Right after graduating from the Yale School of Architecture, Damian worked on a project converting old fish-market buildings in Manhattan's South Street Seaport into residential and retail spaces with the firm that is now COOKFOX Architects. Because the complexity of weaving together various dilapidated centuries-old buildings required an architect to be on site every day, Damian's desk was right in the construction company's office.

Britt was among the first people to rent one of the new apartments. At the time, she had just left the fashion company Ellen Tracy, where she directed the merchandising of brand shops within department stores, like Saks Fifth Avenue and Bloomingdale's, and was freelancing as a stylist for Martha Stewart. It was there in the Seaport that we met, and chance encounters led to deeper discussions ranging from comparisons of our favorite design destinations around the world to the quirks of various projects we were working on. When one of the retail tenants, a pet store named The Salty Paw, needed help outfitting its interior, we decided to tackle it together.

Although we didn't even think about it at the time, that was the moment our studio, and a lifelong relationship, was born. Now, we're the parents of four children—Brecken, Harper, Elliott, and Georgia—and design remains the guiding influence over so many aspects of our lives, whether it's planning a dinner for our friends at our country house in Dutchess County, New York; updating Harper's bedroom as she grows into a teenager; or simply organizing our entrance hall in the city. After we've been discussing the design of projects in the studio all day long, our conversations in the evenings switch to how we can use design to enhance our own lives—and after growing up immersed in design, our kids are more than happy to get in on those discussions, too.

We take architecture and design seriously, understand that buildings and rooms really need to perform their intended functions, and are obsessive about getting even the tiniest details right. But we're also adamant that the end result shouldn't look or feel too serious. All of our work stems from a few guiding beliefs: that design is deeply personal, that it should express something about the people who will use the space, that it should be completely welcoming—and that it should have a little fun.

In many of our projects, you'll see clean lines and pared-down details, but we're no monastic minimalists. A home's interior should be comforting and welcoming, serve as a place to recharge, and directly support the lifestyle someone wants to live. If achieving those objectives requires a few extra pillows or a thought-provoking art installation, we embrace those additions. This line of thinking is one of the reasons that no Studio DB project looks the same as another—each is customized to reflect and serve the people who live and work there.

As we continue on this journey, one of our firm's strengths has been that we, Britt and Damian, come from distinctly different creative backgrounds, and don't always immediately agree on matters of style. Damian grew up in New York with an architect father and a fashion designer mother. But his dad wasn't some corporate architect. In addition to working in historic preservation and pushing for many of the zoning changes that allowed artists to occupy old industrial lofts, he designed inflatable structures in the 1970s that pushed the envelope in literally building shelters from air. The loft that he bought for himself as a place to build those experimental structures, in Manhattan's Union Square, has had many lives. As his own family expanded, he transformed it into more of a residence, piece by piece. It's no wonder Damian caught the architecture bug early on.

Britt grew up in Michigan, and always embraced her wild side. For years, she was a professional snowboarder, and in her late teens she moved to Colorado to participate in halfpipe, boardercross, slopestyle, and big air competitions. But even though she relished catching air and floating through waist-deep powder, she felt a gnawing sense that she had missed her calling. She became increasingly interested in the ways people's surroundings affect how they live. Shortly after moving to New York City, where she initially worked in fashion, she enrolled in interior design studies at the Fashion Institute of Technology.

Today, those different backgrounds continue to serve us well. Even though we work together almost every day, we don't always see eye to eye and still have our own ideas and preferences. Damian brings the rigor of an architect's mind to our projects, and Britt always has her eye on softness, color, and pattern. This results in healthy, sometimes intense, debate and collaboration, because we aren't scared to challenge each other's assumptions. We believe that this willingness to engage in discussion, and to try to see things through each other's eyes, ultimately leads to stronger work.

As we've gained experience and realized more projects together, we've also come to appreciate deeply the art of building. Drawings on paper don't mean much if they're impossible to build. We've been very fortunate to develop a network of builders, artisans, and fabricators who can help bring our most audacious dreams to life. When Studio DB started, we worked in a hands-on way. We literally built the kitchen cabinets in one of our first projects in the Hamptons. For another project, we commissioned our very first employee, Kate Gray, who happened to be taking pottery classes, to make the ceramic tiles we used. Building cabinetry and fabricating ceramics ourselves wasn't our goal but we were happy to do whatever it took to realize our larger vision.

That practical aspect of building, and our continuing wonder at the magic of creation, continues to inform our relationships with our many collaborators. Architects can sometimes get a bad reputation for being hard-nosed and uncompromising when faced with problems or unexpected site conditions, but we approach builders as partners rather than adversaries. Many of the woodworkers, steelworkers, weavers, and wallpaper manufacturers have become longtime friends, having collaborated with us since Studio DB's earliest days.

It's now deeply rewarding to see those relationships flourish on a new level. When we started, we were relatively young and inexperienced and looked to many of these artisans for their expertise. Now that we're more seasoned, we've learned something else: every talented artisan knows their craft so well that they have plenty of ideas and secrets to share. So, as we move from design on paper into production, we listen carefully to our partners and try to stoke their creative energy. It's not just about implementing our ideas; it's about figuring out how our visions can tie together. It's very much a two-way street. We push the artisans we work with to go beyond their comfort zones, and to produce works that are perhaps larger or more intricate than anything they've done before to create interiors that are truly special. But once a project begins, the creative doors are thrown open. One great early example was our collaboration with the lighting company Apparatus, founded by our friends Jeremy

Pages 8–9, 10, and 11: Views of the Studio DB interior near Union Square in New York City.

Opposite: Damian and Britt Zunino in the kitchen of their Manhattan loft.

Anderson and Gabriel Hendifar. Shortly after Apparatus had launched its first collection, we fell in love with its Cloud chandelier, which suspended a canopy of frosted glass globes from a single rod. We wanted to use it in a double-height living room we were designing, but worried it would get lost in the expansive space, so we asked them if they could scale the whole fixture up in size. At first, the company's glassblower said the globes simply couldn't be made any larger. But we all continued to ruminate, until the concept was realized. The result was a dramatic chandelier that was central to the design of that space, and one that became a permanent addition to the Apparatus catalog, as the Cloud XL.

That is far from the only example of collaboration that has led to mutually beneficial results. Our work with artisans and manufacturers has frequently opened up new avenues for everyone involved. With Beni Rugs, we designed the largest Moroccan rug the company had ever produced, which was a source of pride among the weavers. With Calico Wallpaper, the boutique mural-focused company run by our friends Nick and Rachel Cope, our work together led to the creation of Supernova, a range of abstract celestial designs that is now part of its collection.

All this effort highlights something else we have long believed: architecture isn't just about building shelters that can withstand the elements, and interior design isn't just about creating functional spaces to cook, eat, and sleep. At their best, both involve crafting completely new environments: spaces that feel like worlds of their own, where every last detail has been considered to offer a rewarding experience. When you look at things through this lens, every detail, no matter how small—the weight of a door lever in your hand, the way materials transition from one to the other—matters.

As Ludwig Mies van der Rohe famously said, "God is in the details." Or, as Charles Eames put it, "The details are not the details. They make the design." This is why Studio DB will never be the kind of studio that merely hands a set of construction documents off to a builder and walks away. We care too much, and we understand how critical seemingly minor elements can be in realizing a larger vision, so we insist on seeing each project all the way through. For us, every building and interior we design is personal and an opportunity to do something that goes beyond the ordinary.

But at the end of the day, we hope that all the effort put into creating special places simply fades away. We hope people experience and enjoy the spaces we design, and discover specific details over time, rather than seeing evidence of the effort that went into them. The goal is to lift people's spirits, to bring them joy, and, hopefully, to inspire them. They are places to celebrate, not to study the intricacies of different construction methods. Because the most successful design projects, when all is said and done, should support life as you want to live it.

**Opposite:** An unexpected saturation of color for a living room in Greenwich, Connecticut.

**Following pages:** A library in Connecticut playfully lacquered in Varsity Blues by Benjamin Moore.

# PLAYFULLY
# ELEVATED

Do you enjoy staying at luxurious hotels; getting inspired by breath-taking new art, film, or literature; and simply letting your hair down and having a little fun? Well, so do we. And there is no reason your home can't support all these activities on a daily basis. Too often, the field of architecture can seem a little too serious. It can get bogged down in dogma, where the idea of realizing some perfect concept ends up overriding experiential elements, such as warmth and comfort. But if architects can sometimes be faulted for paring things down a little too much, some interior designers go in exactly the opposite direction when attempting to create rooms that look opulent. They add layer upon layer of decorative detail, creating suffocating spaces that only end up feeling fussy.

When we see spaces that don't really work—because they're too rigorous or too embellished—we usually think that the architect or designer forgot something important along the way: the occupants. When residential design is used to express a designer's own agenda or to be published as a showcase of their talents, the desires and personalities of the owners sometimes get pushed to the background. Many of our projects at Studio DB end up being photogenic, but we never begin by thinking about a project as a canvas for our own expression. Each one is truly a collaborative effort, and we encourage our clients to embrace the things that will really make them happy.

Do you want a home with a video arcade? Let's do it. Do you love showstopping art but worry it won't work in your home? We'll find a place for it. Do you want a playroom or child's bedroom that has a sense of fun but still comes off as sophisticated? Now you're speaking our language.

Luxury doesn't have to mean abandoning color, pattern, and playful elements in search of a sober environment—unless that's what someone wants. We'd much rather design a home that caters to an individual's every desire, showcases their personal history and interests, and inspires joy every time they come home. To us, that is true luxury.

# A
# TUDOR
# TRANSFORMED

# Montclair — New Jersey

In life, it's always good to follow your heart. And if you accidentally purchased the wrong home, it doesn't mean you should stay there and try to force yourself to like it. Although it might be difficult to admit it, it's sometimes better to move on.

This is what happened with film director Ruben Fleischer and his wife, Holly Shakoor Fleischer, a former Hollywood publicist turned producer and podcaster, who asked us to renovate their new family home in Montclair. They had recently moved in, with their two young daughters. The couple had already done some work on the house with another designer before deciding to go in a different direction and hiring us to finish the job. We went through the entire design process, but while there were many new elements Ruben and Holly thought they'd like, there was something about the house and property that just didn't feel right for them.

Just as we were about to begin construction, they came to an important conclusion: it wasn't worth doing so much work if they weren't going to love living there. They found a different house nearby and asked us to look at it with them—it was a better, bigger house on a beautiful property with landscaping that had originally been designed by Frederick Law Olmsted. All of us loved it. They bought it, sold the other house, and restarted the design process with a blank page.

The architectural bones of the 10,000-square-foot Tudor Revival house, which was built in 1908, were still intact. However, the home had served as a designer show house a few years earlier and, strangely, the previous owner decided to keep it that way, so there was no sense of cohesion. The dining room was overwhelmed by a full-size faux elephant's head mounted on the wall, the living room walls were done in stripes, and other rooms were wrapped in hand-painted floral murals. Clearly, none of those elements could stay. We stripped out those newer elements while retaining the rooms' original details and gave the house a completely new, consistent vibe.

In a reflection of Ruben and Holly's never-ending search for adventure and fun and their embrace of contemporary art, we lightened up the formal living room with sculptural furniture, like an asymmetrical velvet-covered boomerang sofa atop a shaggy patchwork Moroccan rug from Beni Rugs (it was the largest rug the company had ever made, and we personally traveled to Morocco to inspect it on the loom). In the dining room, we resurfaced the fireplace surround with custom watery-blue glazed tile, painted the original woodwork deep midnight blue, and added floral wallpaper that played off the Kehinde Wiley painting that we planned to hang in the room. Then, because the family loves playing together, we created a video arcade for their vintage machines, an art-making room, and a Lego-building room, in addition to his-and-hers offices.

Anyone expecting a traditional Tudor might think we went too far. But for Ruben and Holly, and their family and friends, the universal reaction has been the opposite: they absolutely love it, because it feels like home.

**Preceding page:** A chair from DeMuro Das swathed in fabric from Dedar in the paneled gallery.

**Opposite:** In the second-floor hallway, wallpaper by Josh Greene Design and a rug by Temple Studio serve as a graphic backdrop for a colorful chair and stool-table, both from Marni, and art by Wyatt Hersey.

**Preceding pages:** Contemporary art and furniture animate the house's original mahogany-paneled walls in the gallery.

**Opposite:** A custom-made brass bar occupies a niche off the dining room.

**Pages 32–33:** Artwork by Kehinde Wiley and an antique Chinese Art Deco rug visually anchor the dramatic dining room.

**Preceding pages:** A mohair-covered vintage sectional sofa by M. Fillmore Harty and a Macaron chair by Gal Gaon for Nilufar in the living room.

**Above:** An Up 50 armchair and ottoman by Gaetano Pesce rest on a custom-designed rug from Beni Rugs.

**Opposite:** A Sideways Sofa by Rikke Frost faces the fireplace.

**Opposite:** The plant-filled music room is painted in Soft Satin by Benjamin Moore.

**Page 40:** A mix of stained and painted wood cabinets in the pantry.

**Page 41:** A wall of art, hung salon style, and Flotation Suspension lamp by Ingo Maurer in the breakfast nook.

**Opposite:** A Wood Totem floor lamp by Allied Maker contrasts with the original pendant light fixture in the stairwell.

**Page 44:** Floral wallpaper by House of Hackney and art in a guest bathroom.

**Page 45:** A custom-made piñata by Confetti System and a headboard upholstered in fabric from Imogen Heath in one of the children's bedrooms.

**Above:** The video arcade with Mixed Tape wallpaper by Rebel Walls.

**Opposite:** The family's screening room is imbued with dark navy.

**First Floor**

1. Gallery
2. Living Room
3. Music Room
4. Photo Booth
5. Bar
6. Dining Room
7. Pantry
8. Kitchen
9. Breakfast Nook
10. Vestibule
11. Mud Room
12. Stair Hall
13. Study

**Second Floor**

1. Gallery
2. Sun Porch
3. Primary Bathroom
4. Primary Bedroom
5. Primary Closet
6. Child's Bedroom
7. Child's Bedroom
8. Homework Room
9. Lego Room
10. Study
11. Laundry Room
12. Stair Hall
13. Guest Bedroom

**Third Floor**

1. Arcade
2. Screening Room
3. Play Nook
4. Bunk Room
5. Playroom
6. Stair Hall
7. Art Room

First Floor

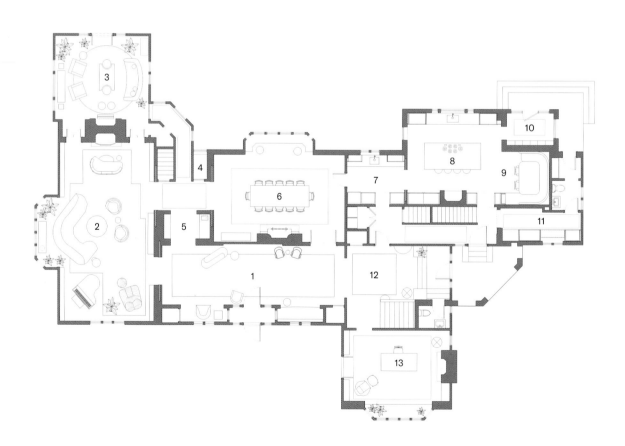

Second Floor

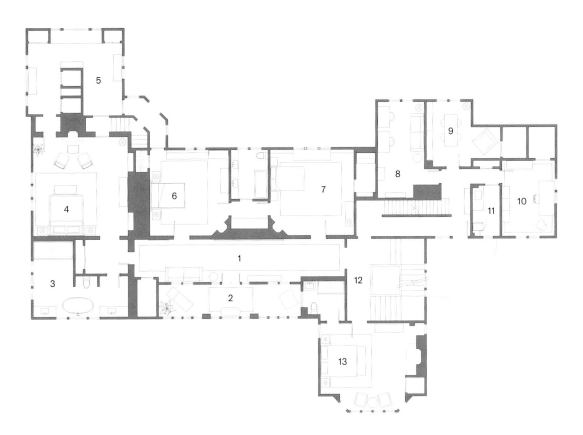

Third Floor

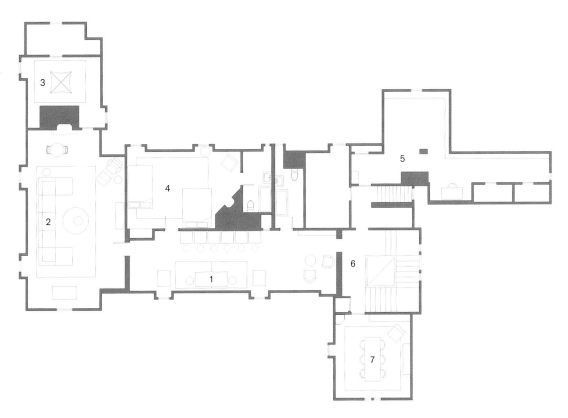

# OUR
# HOME
# UPSTATE

# Dutchess County — New York

Living in New York City is intense, exciting, hectic, and nonstop. But we absolutely love it. We can directly brainstorm with the designers in our studio, visit a client project, attend an exhibition opening, and go out for a fabulous meal—all in a single day. However, sometimes we do need a little pause to catch our breath. For that, there are few places we would rather go than our country home in Dutchess County, New York, which is about a two-hour drive north of the city.

To say this house is a passion project would be an understatement. We built it nearly a decade ago, when Studio DB was still just a scrappy firm with a handful of employees. We began by buying a big empty lot and dreaming. When a site is truly a blank slate, there's a lot of pressure to get the design of a house right—and that's doubly true when it's an architect and designer's own home.

Over the next few years, we put more than half a dozen designs on paper, but we kept having babies and none of the concepts we developed seemed perfect. Damian was envisioning a modernist compound; Britt wanted something with a little more local character. But after many false starts we found our ideal design: a three-story house with a concrete base that's partially buried in a hill, and a structure with the outline of a gable roof on top.

Because money was tight and we wanted the house built with strict attention to detail, Damian served as our general contractor and had the framework of the house prefabricated as structural insulated panels that were assembled on site with a crane in less than three weeks. He also built some of the house himself, from framing interior walls to completing paint touchups, while managing subcontractors such as electricians and plumbers. Of course, even once the house was substantially complete, work never stopped. Every year, it seems we take on a new project. We added a pool; we keep expanding the gardens; we clear brush to open up more of the views. We even have plans to rig up a rope tow to turn our hill into a little ski slope.

Life at the house is free, easy, and peaceful. It's a complete escape from our lives in the city and where we envision our kids coming to gather when they're older. To put it in the simplest of terms: it's our home.

**Preceding page:** The house blends with the natural surroundings, with lush greenery inside and out and views framed by the punched openings in the facade.

**Opposite:** The view from the green roof to the pool and rolling hills beyond.

**Pages 54–55:** Britt and Damian's girls in the house's courtyard, with beloved horses from Hope Rising Farm.

**Preceding page:** The living room, with a vintage Costela sofa designed by Martin Eisler and Carlo Hauner in the foreground, is open to nature on both sides.

**Above:** The dining room table with a tablecloth of Dutch wax-print fabric from Vlisco and chairs from Michael Robbins.

**Opposite:** A collage by New York–based collaborative Ghost of a Dream hangs above a Lake Low credenza from BDDW.

Page 60: A Wood sconce in walnut from Blue Green Works is to the left of the kitchen hood, which is clad in hand-painted tiles from BDDW.

Preceding page: A print by Wassaic Project artist Taha Clayton hangs behind a lamp from Dumais Made on the bar cart.

Opposite: A moody Alskar rug from Marc Phillips contrasts with the clean lines of the bed from Suite NY in a child's bedroom.

**Above:** Glow-in-the-dark Perseid wallpaper from Flat Vernacular covers the ceiling of a children's bedroom.

**Opposite:** Nuvole al Tramonto wallpaper from Fornasetti provides a magical backdrop in a child's bedroom.

**Page 66:** A freestanding bathtub from MTI provides a rare moment of calm.

**Page 67:** The airy primary suite is layered with a photograph by Jeff Barnett-Winsby, a Moroccan rug, and a bedspread in a Nickey Kehoe textile.

**Lower Level**

1. Garage
2. Mechanical Room
3. Game Room
4. Family Room
5. Laundry Room
6. Guest Bedroom

**First Floor**

1. Foyer
2. Mudroom
3. Pantry
4. Kitchen
5. Dining Room
6. Living Room
7. Child's Bedroom
8. Child's Bedroom
9. Child's Bedroom
10. Courtyard

**Second Floor**

1. Primary Closet
2. Primary Bathroom
3. Primary Bedroom
4. Study
5. Roof Deck

Lower Level

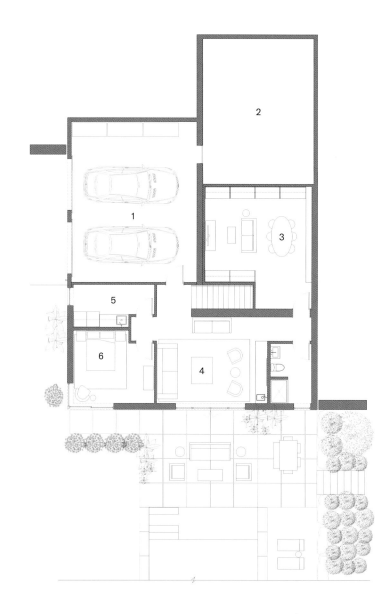

First Floor

Second Floor

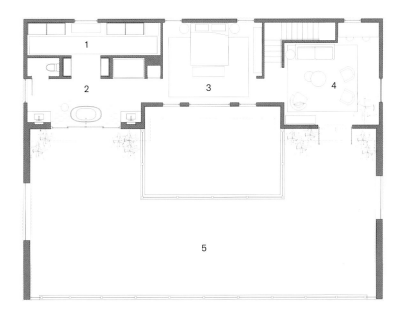

# THE
# LOFT
# WE LOVE

# Greenwich Village, Manhattan — New York

Our house in Dutchess County might be our restful escape, but our home in Manhattan is the place our family counts on when experiencing all the urban things we love—engaging work and school, a big circle of friends involved in creative pursuits, and endless encounters, both planned and unexpected, with people who delight and inspire us.

This particular loft is packed with personal history. Damian's father purchased it in 1970 when it was just commercial space packed with manufacturers and artists, and he used it as a production studio for his explorations in inflatable architecture. When he married Damian's mother, and children arrived, he slowly transformed parts of it into a home. There were always things to climb, strange stairways and different fort-like spaces to explore. Damian spent his entire childhood sleeping in a Murphy bed installed below a maze of climbing lofts.

When Damian was studying architecture in college, the loft changed again, as his parents renovated to make it a little more residential still. To help with that renovation, Damian applied his new computer-aided design skills to develop the plans, effectively making it his first project. For years afterward, we watched the loft continue to evolve, as we got together for holidays and family meals. Then, as time passed, Damian's parents began spending more time in Connecticut and Florida. When Covid arrived, his parents invited us to move into the loft, since they were rarely there. We did, and soon after we relocated our studio to our current location near Union Square, just a few blocks away.

Living in the loft was originally supposed to be temporary, but we never left. After we settled in, we began seeing a few little things that needed to be updated. But once we broke out the tools, it didn't take us long to slide into a full-blown renovation—after all, that's what we do. We replaced the windows (most of which didn't open), installed air conditioning so the interior didn't bake in the summer, and repaired a bathroom that had leaked into our downstairs neighbor's apartment. Before long, we were also overhauling the kitchen and putting in new floors. Now, it really feels like it's ours.

Because of that, we were worried Damian's parents would be upset when they saw it for the first time. Homes are so personal, especially ones with elements you've designed and built yourself. But when they came for that first dinner, they absolutely loved it. They were so excited for us and their grandchildren to be living in the space, and they viewed our project as a continuation of their own work. This home contains a lot of history—but the story is still being written.

**Preceding page:** The Wanderlust mural from Calico and tile from clé in the foyer.

**Opposite:** The quirky design, including the step-up bathroom, evolved over decades.

**Pages 74–75:** A prototype Sev-Drulo sectional from BDDW and Moroccan rugs provide comfort in the living room.

**Preceding pages:** An asymmetrical burnished-brass island reflects the kitchen's unusual floor plan.

**Opposite:** A vintage George Nelson–designed desk resides in a library fit for an architect, originally planned by Damian's father.

**Pages 80–81:** The primary bedroom, washed in Setting Plaster from Farrow & Ball, features lighting from J. M. Szymanski and Apparatus.

**Page 82:** The casual den, with artwork by David Shrigley: Untitled "When Life Gives You a Lemon"

**Page 83:** A warm and playful child's bedroom.

# A PUNCHY PREWAR CO-OP

# Upper West Side, Manhattan — New York

When a young family outgrew their tiny apartment in downtown Manhattan, they found a larger co-op unit in a prewar building on the Upper West Side. It came with all the traditional details you would expect, including beamed ceilings, crown molding, and tall baseboards. After years of wear and tear, however, it needed a refresh, and this couple didn't want to just re-create what had always been there. They are passionate collectors of contemporary art and midcentury modern furniture, and they wanted somewhere they could really display those pieces in an impactful way.

The directive was to respect the building's history but make the interior bold. We started by demolishing many of the small rooms and tiny closets, so common in prewar buildings, to make the spaces lighter and brighter. Then, we built on the period details while bringing in the drama. In the living room, we retained the original fireplace but added graphic Calacatta Viola marble for the hearth and surround, coated the ceilings in high-gloss lacquer, and installed panel molding on the walls to frame their art while adding a purposely imperfect layered look that seems like it developed over time.

In the dining room, we went in the opposite direction: painting the ceiling deep blue and lining the walls with navy-and-gold wallpaper. On one wall, we installed a concealed bar that lights up with sunset-inspired orangey ombré wallpaper when you pull open the door.

The rest of the apartment continues this sense of discovery. The entrance hall ceiling is covered with marbleized wallpaper. The powder room is wrapped in colorful flowers and has a sink crafted from stunning green-and-white stone. Where an existing column could have ruined our plans for an expanded kitchen, we chose to celebrate it by adding shelving lined with colorful glassware. The one room where we dialed things down was the primary bedroom, where they wanted a more relaxed, serene vibe and we embraced a palette of off-whites and soft pinks. It's a personal family home that embraces the unexpected.

**Preceding page:** A wallpaper mural from Rebel Walls in a child's bedroom.

**Opposite:** A contemporary painting by Hilary Pecis contrasts with the historic detailing of the mantelpiece.

**Pages 88–89:** Bold colors and forms populate the art-filled living room.

Page 90: Grass-cloth wallpaper from Calico is a sunny surprise in the bar.

Preceding page: A custom tronchi glass chandelier from High Style Deco and a painting by Mel Bochner in the dramatic dining room.

Above: Josef Frank–designed wallpaper from Svenskt Tenn and a vanity in Cipollino Ondulato marble enliven a powder room.

Opposite: Slender shelves make the most of an immovable column in the kitchen.

# EXACTING
# APPROACHABILITY

Anyone who looks at our work, or steps into a room we've designed, can tell that we're sticklers for detail. We don't design interiors that are "close enough" or simply hope for the best when our clients' homes are under construction. While every project begins with a big, overarching vision for what we want to achieve, our process then moves on to working out every single detail—and we really do mean every detail. In our eyes, encountering buildings and rooms that look interesting from a distance but appear careless when you get up close is always a missed opportunity.

For a project to really sing, every fine point needs to be considered. We're obsessive about the way a cabinet pull feels under your fingertips, how flooring and wall finishes transition seamlessly from one room to the next, and the way that lighting can dramatically change your impression of a space. And although we respect and preserve traditional details when working in historic houses, our work tends to skew more modern, where there are far fewer trim pieces to hide imperfections.

We know we're not alone, of course. Many modern architects focus on the same things—the perfectly square white walls, the floor-to-ceiling expanses of glass, and the crisp sense of newness. But sometimes that means missing opportunities to play up more human elements. In the quest for perfection, homes sometimes end up feeling cold and impersonal. They are containers that might be nice to admire but where few people want to stay for long.

When we see interiors that are stripped down to just the essentials, we can't help but feel like they're full of unrealized potential. If only someone had pushed a little further, and hadn't been frightened of what a few personal elements would have done to the clean-lined architecture, we think, they might have created truly breathtaking rooms.

That's why even though we're always focused on realizing intricate design details, we're also committed to making space for the softer, wabi-sabi touches that make a house a home. We like to think of it as a more human take on modernism. Even as we design contemporary houses, we embrace lessons from the past and the evidence of craftsmanship created by hand, rather than trying to erase them. Ultimately, our goal is to design spaces that feel approachable and livable, and are simply a joy to be in.

**Page 95:** A sinuous custom sofa and a Synapse pendant from Apparatus embody the potentials of a small space in our room for the Kips Bay Decorator Show House.

**Opposite:** A tiny, but luxurious, bar and a mural by de Gournay.

# AN
# ESCAPE
# IN THE
# HAMPTONS

# Southampton — New York

This home began with the house next door. Our clients, the same people who had us design the Tribeca warehouse apartment (see pages 124–45), were looking for a new getaway in the Hamptons and went to see a new house a builder had constructed to sell. They loved the location and could see that it was meticulously built. They were tempted to buy it—but then they saw another opportunity.

There was an empty lot right next door. Instead of buying a ready-made house, they could invest in designing their own, they realized, and create a house that reflected their needs, desires, and personalities. They bought the lot, tapped us and local architect Raymond Renault to collaborate on the design of a brand-new house from scratch, and recruited the same builder to construct it.

Right from the beginning, they knew what they wanted. The house needed to be a family home, with room for everyone, and plenty of space for having fun, indoors and out. They wanted it to feel relaxed and beachy, but in a way that was interesting and unexpected rather than cliché. And they wanted a worry-free place that could withstand wet swimsuits and sandy feet while still projecting a sense of elegance.

The result is an expansive home based on a simple gable-roofed structure lined in Alaskan yellow cedar, bronze-hued metal, and plenty of glass that connects to a smaller gable-roofed pool house. Inside the front door, the entrance hall opens to a glassy, sun-drenched, double-height living room hung with Lindsey Adelman chandeliers recalling barnacles. Throughout the house, we chose distinctive varieties of natural materials, such as Ceppo di Gré limestone, which has the look of oversized terrazzo, and white oak for floors and wall panels, as well as metals with an accelerated sense of age, such as patinated bronze, burnished brass, and verdigris copper, which look as though they have spent a lifetime by the sea.

It's a home that invites discovery and exploration. As friends and family move between the dining room, library, and family room, as well as outdoor gathering places like the firepit and pool, each feels like its own unique destination. It's a beach house where everyone can be together when they choose, but people also have the space for moments of quiet contemplation when they need it.

**Preceding page:** Ceppo di Gré limestone and white oak paneling clad the foyer, which features an entry table by House of Badami and a mirror by Chen Chen & Kai Williams.

**Opposite:** Charred cypress paneling from reSAWN TIMBER in the bathroom of the pool pavilion.

**Page 102:** A constellation of verdigris light fixtures by Allied Maker illuminates the covered terrace.

**Page 103:** A view of the pool pavilion illustrates the interconnection between interior and exterior spaces.

Preceding pages: A conversation circle of custom Pouf Arc sofas from Stahl + Band in the living room is anchored by a pair of Isla tables by Egg Collective.

Right: Art by Jacob Hashimoto with a bespoke dining table by Tim Vranken.

Page 108: A custom banquette, chairs from Crump & Kwash, and a pendant light from Blue Green Works at the breakfast table.

Page 109: Art by Ruby Sky Stiler in the family room, a monochromatic retreat.

**Preceding pages:** A Cerine Swagged Chandelier from Trueing and a custom verdigris range hood in the kitchen.

**Above:** A stained white oak bathtub offers breathtaking views from the primary bathroom.

**Opposite:** Wild Grasses wallpaper from de Gournay in the primary bedroom.

**Pages 114–15:** Oyster White marble and verdigris pendants from Allied Maker in the primary bathroom.

**Above:** Playfully patterned tile from Elisa Passino Studio and Breccia Antica marble in a child's bathroom.

**Opposite:** Botanic Glasscloth wallpaper and a hand-painted lantern from Caitlin McGauley in the adjoining bedroom.

**Pages 118–19:** A gridded wall with insets of fabric from Rebecca Atwood and sconces from Blueprint Lighting in the boy's bedroom.

**Pages 120–21:** Tile from Smink Studio finishes a guest bathroom, which has an expansive view.

**First Floor**

1. Foyer
2. Jr. Primary Bedroom
3. Family Room
4. Living Room
5. Dining Room
6. Wine Hall
7. Kitchen
8. Pantry
9. Mudroom & Laundry
10. Guest Bedroom
11. Main Stair Hall
12. Sun Room
13. Pool Cabana Lounge
14. Golf Simulator

**Second Floor**

1. Stair Hall
2. Mezzanine
3. Primary Closets
4. Primary Bathroom
5. Primary Bedroom
6. Child's Bedroom
7. Child's Bedroom
8. Guest Bedroom
9. Guest Bedroom
10. Fitness Room
11. Sun Deck

**Third Floor**

1. Library
2. Office
3. Playroom
4. Homework Nook
5. Bunk Room
6. Roof Deck

First Floor

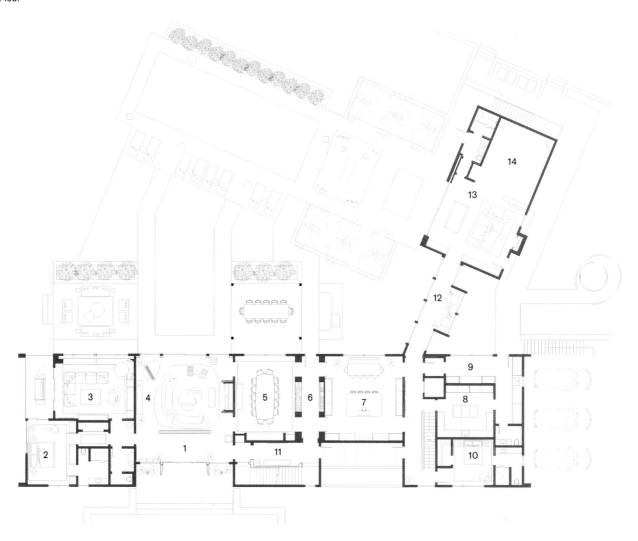

Second Floor

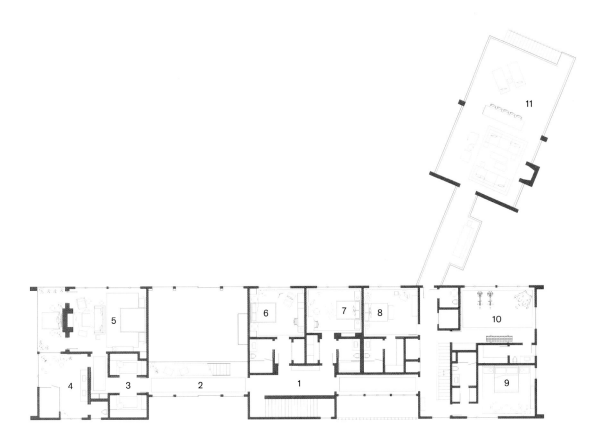

Third Floor

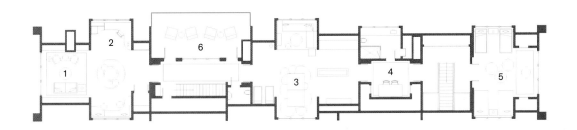

# A TRIBECA WAREHOUSE TRANSFORMED

# Tribeca, Manhattan — New York

Some families are so busy that it's difficult for them to focus on the design of their homes. The parents travel for work, the kids need to be shepherded to school and extracurricular activities, and renovation plans fall by the wayside. When this family of four bought a fully furnished apartment in a 1915 Tribeca warehouse in the early 2010s, they looked at it as a temporary measure—a move-in-ready home where they could live until they got around to making it their own.

Five years later, they hadn't changed much when the unit next door went up for sale. Already short on space, they knew that a similar opportunity might never present itself again, so they pounced and bought it. And once they closed, there was no more delaying things—the only way to make sensible use of the two adjacent apartments was to renovate and blow out the walls in between them. That's when they contacted us.

Combining apartments is a surprisingly common activity in New York, but any-one who has done it can tell you there are many quirks that need to be addressed. Small rooms need to be merged into larger spaces. Circulation paths need to be rethought. Extra kitchens need to be removed. And entry sequences have to be defined. That's challenging in any building, but especially so in one that's more than one hundred years old and was originally designed as a storage space.

Nevertheless, after extensive demolition, we managed to create a cohesive apart-ment that wraps around the building's two internal courtyards. At the center of the home is a large, wide-open living-and-dining room lined with sunny windows. This space flows right into the kitchen, where a breakfast nook is only partially enclosed by a screen of blackened steel and reeded glass.

When we encountered existing elements that others might have seen as problems, we simply solved things in playful ways. In a reclaimed hallway where there was a column right in the middle of the circulation route, we created an entry foyer with a striped concrete floor and a big upholstered bench that wraps around the post. At the main entrance door, where there was a window looking out into other apartments, we designed a leggy oak-and-brass console with an integrated mirror and placed it before a sheer curtain to provide privacy without blocking the light. And where it was impossible to run new plumbing to a soaking tub in the primary bedroom, we designed a sinuous platform finished in troweled concrete to make it an intentional feature.

Along the way, the owners became so interested in design that they began collecting furniture by new American designers, including glass coffee tables by John Hogan and metal tables by J. M. Szymanski. When the apartment was finished, they were ready for more. Almost immediately, they asked us to undertake another project with them—a new weekend house in the Hamptons, built from the ground up. For an architect and designer, that might just be the ultimate compliment.

**Preceding page:** In the open kitchen, a curved waterfall detail on the island mirrors the archway and barrel-vaulted ceilings.

**Opposite:** The vintage Togo sofa by Ligne Roset and Polycade video-game system set up the playroom for fun.

**Pages 128–29:** The living room highlights the work of American designers, including a sofa from Egg Collective, tables from John Hogan and J. M. Szymanski, daybed from Coil + Drift, and lighting from Apparatus.

**Above:** A striped concrete-tile floor, built-in bench, and Moon Light by Ben & Aja Blanc in the foyer.

**Opposite:** A pared-down powder room with a blue calcite vanity and vintage pendant light by Carlo Nason for Mazzega.

**Page 132:** A Meteor pendant by Christopher Boots over the cloudy resin dining table from Wüd Furniture.

**Page 133:** A blackened-steel-and-reeded-glass screen by Argosy Designs defines the breakfast nook.

**Pages 134–35:** Lavender-hued grass cloth and frosted-glass pendants from Gabriel Scott in the primary bedroom.

**Page 136:** A panel of fabric with copper threads from ZAK+FOX, as a backdrop, and a custom console fabricated by Robert Sukrachand create a proper entrance for the apartment.

**Preceding page:** Iceberg White calcite and Celestial Pebble pendants from Ochre by the soaking tub.

**Opposite:** A cozy seating area in the primary bedroom, with a nook upholstered in alpaca bouclé from Rosemary Hallgarten.

**Preceding pages:** The Flora pattern from Calico extends from upholstered headboards to wallpaper to drapery in a child's room.

**Above:** Mystic Lagoon wallpaper by Aimée Wilder and a red faucet from VOLA in a child's bathroom.

**Opposite:** A bookshelf serves as climbing structure to a child's reading loft.

1. Foyer
2. Mudroom
3. Living Room
4. Dining Room
5. Breakfast Nook
6. Kitchen
7. Pantry
8. Playroom
9. Study
10. Guest Bedroom
11. Laundry Room
12. Child's Bedroom
13. Primary Bathroom
14. Primary Closet
15. Primary Bedroom
16. Child's Bedroom

# A CLASSIC MANHATTAN LOFT

# Tribeca, Manhattan — New York

When a family asked for help redesigning their new loft in Manhattan's Tribeca neighborhood, they had clear ideas about how they wanted to live. Previously, they had renovated a whole town house in Brooklyn that spared no expense. But, when they tried settling in with their twins, they found it never felt quite like home. They didn't really enjoy being on separate floors, the main living room ended up seeming a little too formal, and they usually spent all their time together in a small family room by the kitchen.

For the way they wanted to live, they concluded, it made far more sense to move back to Manhattan, and into a wide-open space where they didn't always have to debate which room, and which floor, they wanted to gather on. The apartment they bought was in many ways a classic New York loft in a cast-iron building. It had exposed-brick walls, pressed-tin ceilings, and old industrial-style metal radiators.

Our design for the space kept and celebrated all of these elements, but also tempered the coarseness of those industrial elements with polished details, including meticulously crafted cabinetry with custom wood-and-bronze pulls, and softer elements, such as upholstered wall paneling in the primary bedroom.

One of the biggest challenges was an existing wall of brick arches running straight down the middle of the apartment. But in the end, that existing architectural element turned out to be a blessing. We retained the textural appeal of the brick but de-emphasized the material slightly by whitewashing the bricks and planning sightlines between the various spaces. We also riffed on the arches in a few different playful ways: we designed arch-shaped steel-and-glass doors, wallpapered an arched niche as a headboard wall, and gave some of the custom cabinetry similar curves.

Finished with vibrant colors and patterned tiles, textiles, and art, it's an upscale home that never feels too precious.

**Preceding page:** Vintage furniture, including a chair by T. H. Robsjohn-Gibbings reimagined in a fabric from Imogen Heath, in the entrance hall.

**Opposite:** The eclectic living room, illuminated by a Sarus chandelier by David Weeks.

**Pages 150–51:** A muscular kitchen of marble, oxidized maple, and textured subway tile.

Page 152: A pressed-tin ceiling, brick walls, and red exposed sprinkler pipe in the kitchen.

Preceding page: A set of Ladder chairs from BDDW flank the clients' vintage dining table.

Above: Custom cabinetry, inspired by the loft's brick arches, and wallpaper by Flat Vernacular in a child's bedroom.

Opposite: A playful bathroom with Buggie wallpaper from Abnormals Anonymous and a colorful Pyrolave vanity top.

# A CONNECTED TOWN HOUSE

# Downtown Manhattan — New York

When Studio DB was still just a small firm, with a few compact urban renovations in its portfolio, the owners of this house liked what they saw, enough to entrust us to design our first large-scale project—a complete five-story town house in downtown Manhattan.

We actually felt a little green for the job at the time—a sense that was only amplified at one of our first meetings, when Britt dutifully took off her shoes and discovered she had put on mismatched socks that morning. Some people might have walked away and chosen a different design firm right then. But this couple actually appreciated the mix-up. It was a signal that we weren't too fancy and didn't take ourselves too seriously—we were collaborators they could work with. It allowed them to relax.

Located on a beautiful cobbled street and graced with a traditional cast-iron facade, the 1920 building had a lot going for it. But when it had been converted from a commercial building to a residence years earlier, we felt some opportunities had been missed. Although the floors were linked by a shared staircase, each level was closed off from the others, so it felt almost like five separate spaces rather than one cohesive residence. And all the white and off-white finishes running through the space felt a little tame for the owners.

With the help of one of our favorite builders and our network of craftspeople, we completely opened up the house by giving it an extensive new steel structure, including a steel staircase with a rolled-edge handrail and treads made from individual pieces of reclaimed teak and metal laminated together. On the top floor, we put a glass walkway over joists so sunlight can flood down the stairwell into the entire structure. These changes make the home feel like one continuous space.

Of course, we were just as focused on the smaller details and gave the home personality with elements such as wallpaper based on an antique map of New York Harbor, children's rooms with concealed doors that allowed the spaces to connect, and a roof terrace with a sofa hung from a pergola on ropes, an urban porch swing. It was truly a labor of love for us, and a learning experience that would inform many of the projects that followed.

Page 162: An Endless lamp from Roll & Hill illuminates the kitchen's oxidized maple and lacquered surfaces.

Preceding page: A collection of Sorenthia lights from Studio DUNN in the dining area.

Above: The new staircase with treads made of laminated widths of reclaimed teak and steel.

Opposite: The striking blackened-steel railing structure visually connects the town house's five floors.

Page 166: An upholstered wall in the primary bedroom.

Preceding page: The dressing area, with custom teak closets and a midcentury modern stool upholstered in mohair velvet.

Above: A custom CNC-milled climbing wall with a backlit map of New York City.

Opposite: Custom shelving, accommodating balls for a variety of games, next to the basketball court.

# A HOME FOR A COLLECTOR

# Flatiron District, Manhattan — New York

Every design project is a collaborative effort, but some are more intimate than others. When Andrew Weissmann asked us to design his loft in Manhattan's Flatiron District, we knew there would be deep, good-natured discussion, and push and pull, around every element. That's because in addition to being a high-profile attorney and MSNBC analyst, Andrew is also a natural-born collector with a deep-seated passion for design.

The design brief was to maintain the loft's existing character with its wood columns and muscular moldings, but also to make it work better with interventions that felt appropriate for the space. The ceiling was high, so we suspended a steel loft with rods and turnbuckles to make a library, and connected it to the ground floor with a slender folded steel staircase that takes up a minimal amount of space.

Brake-form steel shelves offer a place for Andrew to store and display not only his extensive book collection, but also a range of intriguing curiosities, including antique cameras and a first-generation iPod. At the entrance to the bedrooms, we added a wood shelving unit with sliding doors to serve as a flexible divider between public and private spaces while also offering a place for another of his collections: a range of white ironstone china.

For ventilation above the kitchen island, we suggested a commercial dust collector rather than a conventional kitchen hood, which is a detail Andrew loved because it amplified the industrial feel of the space. And then we worked together to place his extensive range of vintage furniture, objects, and works of art, which he has spent a lifetime collecting. Many people say they want eclectic interior design—but Andrew really lives it.

**Preceding page:** An industrial dust collector, repurposed as a range hood, in the teak and concrete kitchen.

**Opposite:** A sunny sitting area lush with plants.

**Pages 174–75:** The double-height living space with Isamu Noguchi–designed Freeform sofa and ottoman from Vitra in the foreground.

Opposite: Custom shelving, perfect for the display of white ironstone china, doubles as a room divider.

Page 178: The client's collection of vintage cameras and iPods.

Page 179: A folded-steel staircase and loft suspended by rods and turnbuckles.

# UNEXPECTED
# TRADITIONAL

When it comes to matters of design, most people feel like they have to choose. Are you a minimalist or a maximalist? Do you prefer black or white? Should your home look modern or traditional?

We're firm believers that you shouldn't have to decide. Why not be open to it all, look at design that has come before as a vast library of inspirational references, and simply embrace the things you like? That's what we do. Although we both grew up studying modernism, we dove into design history along the way and are just as enthralled by the brawny architecture of Scottish castles, the intricacies of French Art Deco, and the cozy utility of early American cabins as we are with the work of Le Corbusier and Charlotte Perriand.

Few people stop to think about it, but even the word modern is something of a misnomer. The modernist movement began more than a century ago. While it began as a challenge to the old way of doing things, modernism has been around long enough now that its radical edges have been polished smooth.

Rather than trying to stick to preconceived notions about style, we find it much more interesting not to limit ourselves. We love working in a seventeenth-century palazzo just as much as a twenty-first-century glass condo tower (okay, maybe the palazzo is a little more fun). But we also try to avoid the trap of attempting to mimic history. Yes, we believe it's important to respect the past, and we take pains to preserve and restore a building's most compelling features when working on historic structures, but the world has changed, which means the spaces where we live, love, and laugh should change as well.

Where would you rather spend time: in a space that is a slave to design decisions from a century ago, or one that embraces the past but also reflects your passions? We always choose the latter and believe that leads us to much more interesting places, where originality is allowed to flourish. Ultimately, it's that dialogue, that push and pull between different viewpoints from different eras, that makes the end result more engaging.

# A FILMMAKERS' CREATIVE CLASSIC

# Upper East Side, Manhattan — New York

Working with the documentary film superstars Chai Vasarhelyi and Jimmy Chin on their Upper East Side residence was deeply rewarding. Because they spend months at a time shooting in different locations all over the world, when they were at home in New York, Chai wanted to be close to her parents. The location of the apartment they bought is perfect from that perspective, because it's just around the corner from her parents' town house.

The apartment itself, however, didn't really reflect the way they live. A space of about 3,000 square feet in a Park Avenue building from 1913 that hadn't been touched in decades, it had many appealing features, but it was also a little sedate for adventurers who had built their careers on following thrill seekers to the ends of the Earth.

Another challenge was that Chai and Jimmy don't always agree on matters of interior design. Chai adores fashion and whimsy. In her mind, the more vibrant the color or pattern, the better. Jimmy is more of a minimalist, and prefers letting muscular architectural details tell their own story. Bringing these two visions together might seem impossible, but it's not. It was actually a perfect job for Studio DB, especially because they reminded us a lot of ourselves.

We restored and expanded upon the original details, including the coffered ceilings, crown molding, and chair railing, while adding in new elements of such heft that they look like they might have always been there. The new foyer floor is terrazzo—but it's not terrazzo as you usually see it. In Chai and Jimmy's apartment, we made it with massive chunks of stone slabs and slices of a few choice rocks Jimmy collected while climbing mountains.

We also brought in the color and pattern Chai craved, but in targeted blasts that make sense to both of them. A custom de Gournay scenic mural in the dining room is their favorite. Depicting a mountain range in gold and blue hues, it reflects Jimmy's passion. But when you look closely, you see that a few of the flowers on the trees are actually hot pink: a nod to Chai's focus on creative fun.

In the den, an antique Chinese Art Deco rug, which was the first item we bought for the apartment, led to bold red lacquer and more de Gournay wallpaper, this time depicting mischievous monkeys. But the monkeys looked a little too serious for Chai, so we had them painted with happier faces. More surprises await in the children's rooms, including a cabinet concealing climbing holds that lead up to a suspended rope loft, and magnetic wallpaper with figures and objects that can be changed over time. Chai and Jimmy's Oscars and many other awards are displayed in unexpected locations, such as in the powder room or mixed in with the kids' trophies above the bar.

Everyone who steps through the door gets the message loud and clear: this is anything but a staid traditional home.

**Preceding page:** A Gianfranco Frattini-designed Sesann sofa from Tacchini, vintage Italian chandelier, and *Beach Fade*, a painting by Isca Greenfield-Sanders, in the living room.

**Opposite:** The marble sink blends with a mountainous mural from Pierre Frey in the powder room.

**Pages 188–89:** Chai and Jimmy with their kids, in an eclectic living room that showcases the couple's wide-ranging tastes.

**Above:** A terrazzo floor with massive chunks of multicolored stones in the foyer.

**Opposite:** A cane chandelier is paired with a vintage Italian console and an antique family heirloom chair.

Opposite: Deco Monkeys wallpaper from de Gournay and red-lacquer trim in the den. The Chinese Art Deco rug inspired colors throughout the apartment.

Pages 194–95: In the dining room, Model 71 chairs designed by Niels Otto Møller and a Captain's credenza from BDDW encased in aqua-colored bridle leather.

**Above:** The dining room's hand-painted scenic mural from de Gournay incorporates hot-pink tree blossoms, a customization.

**Opposite:** Shelves at the bar hold some of the couple's many awards, along with children's trophies.

**Above:** Wood-and-metal pulls finish custom cabinets in the kitchen.

**Opposite:** A small breakfast table with woven La Perla chairs by Tucurinca, handcrafted by weavers in Colombia.

**Opposite:** Silk curtains and a mural with gold leaf from Gracie in the primary bedroom.

**Above:** A wardrobe in the form of a playful castle allows for additional storage and fun in a child's room.

**Opposite:** An antique wicker bed provides a dreamy place to sleep.

**Above:** Magnetic wallpaper from Sian Zeng enables scene changes in a bathroom.

**Opposite:** Another child's bedroom, with more opportunities for play and climbing.

1. Vestibule
2. Foyer
3. Kitchen
4. Butler's Pantry
5. Dining Room
6. Living Room
7. Screening Room
8. Child's Bedroom
9. Child's Bedroom
10. Primary Bedroom
11. Primary Closet
12. Primary Bathroom
13. Primary Closet
14. Guest Bedroom
15. Laundry Room

# A RELAXED PARK AVENUE PAD

# Upper East Side, Manhattan — New York

When a family asked for help reimagining their classic 1920s Park Avenue apartment, their interest in design was clear. We had similar views on so many matters of style. They had lived in the apartment for years and had filled it with tasteful furniture, fabrics, wallpaper, and accessories. If anything, their problem was that they had collected too many things. What they needed was assistance with setting out a clear vision for the space, and thoughtful editing to create a cohesive design.

Our work began with a considered reorganization of the spaces. Apartments designed in the 1920s reflect a way of living that no longer makes sense for a lot of families. This apartment had a formal living room and dining room that were barely being used, a tiny closed kitchen, and bedrooms that were accessed by two different, disjointed circulation paths that simply wasted space. We corrected those issues by expanding and opening up the kitchen to the adjoining rooms and reclaiming some of the old circulation space to make larger bedrooms for the children. Park Avenue co-ops are famously strict when it comes to moving plumbing, so we repurposed an existing bathroom to give each child a private sink and water closet that connects to a shared shower with lockable frosted-glass doors in between.

Then, we mixed contemporary and traditional details, and serious and whimsical moments. To make a much more inviting dining room, we installed a de Gournay chinoiserie-inspired mural above a cushy banquette that wraps around two sides of the space, inviting family members and guests to dine or simply hang out. As a counterpoint to that traditional mural, we installed the Shape Up series of suspended lamps by Ladies & Gentlemen Studio, with different geometric forms above a custom dining table with legs painted bright red.

In the living room, we lacquered the ceiling glossy white to pull sunlight deep into the space, then added curvaceous furniture that is more playful than formal, including vintage Vladimir Kagan chairs, a scooped bamboo coffee table, and a custom brass-and-oak media unit with radiused corners. A concealed door opens to reveal another unexpected touch: a tiny bar finished in wavy wallpaper and coral paint. The end result is a dynamic home that caters to one family's way of living rather than blindly following convention.

Preceding page: A mural from de Gournay and the Shape Up series of suspended lamps by Ladies & Gentlemen Studio in the dining area.

Opposite: A custom banquette echoes the built-in seating at the dining table.

Pages 212–13: A high-gloss ceiling brightens the living room.

**Above:** Curved corners and an inlaid green-leather top in the custom cabinetry.

**Opposite:** A pair of Tripod lounge chairs by Vladimir Kagan sits atop a Scallop rug in abaca from Patterson Flynn.

**Above:** Vintage German flower sconces enhance the mural in the dining area.

**Opposite:** A flush door conceals the secret living-room bar.

**Pages 218–19:** The kitchen opens to the rest of the apartment with large pocket doors, an architectural intervention.

**Opposite:** Feather Bloom Sisal wallpaper by Schumacher and a custom vanity in Arabescato marble adorn the powder room.

**Page 222:** In the peaceful primary bedroom, one of a pair of sconces by Jennifer Wall from the Urban Electric Company.

**Page 223:** The primary bathroom, detailed in brass and mosaic marble tile.

**Above:** A vanity for a teenager, with a shaggy sheepskin stool and Biami wallpaper from Eskayel.

**Opposite:** A custom bed that combines storage with sleeping space.

1. Foyer
2. Dining Room
3. Kitchen
4. Family Room
5. Study
6. Laundry Room
7. Living Room
8. Bar
9. Primary Bathroom
10. Primary Bedroom
11. Primary Closet
12. Child's Bedroom
13. Child's Bedroom

# A HOME FOR ARTISTS AND SURFERS

# Boerum Hill, Brooklyn — New York

When our dear friends—artist Christopher Daniels and his wife, Alice Daniels, the vice president of creative services at Vera Wang—needed an escape from Manhattan's SoHo (where we had designed a loft for them) as they began to start a family, they didn't have to look far. The Boerum Hill section of Brooklyn offered just the sort of friendly, relaxed neighborhood they desired.

With our help, they began looking at town houses. When we saw a classic, red-brick town house from 1899 with tall, slender windows on a street with mature trees, we knew it had potential. Sure, it was a wreck inside, with extensive water damage and ceilings featuring gorgeous plasterwork that were beginning to cave in, but it didn't take long for all of us to agree that this was the place.

Over the following months, we stripped the house down to the brick walls and rough-hewn framing before painstakingly building it back up. We took pieces of the original moldings and had new plaster knives made so the ceiling medallions and details could be reproduced. We added antique wood floors and designed simple Shaker-style built-ins, as well as minimalist clean-lined bookcases in the living room that terminate at an ornate baseboard. Christopher brought in weathered mantelpieces that his family had collected in Virginia, which provided an immediate sense of age.

To furnish the space, Alice and Christopher collaborated with his sister, interior designer Courtnay Daniels, who added to the sense of timeless comfort. The completed town house appears distinguished but never takes itself too seriously. With an art collection that cuts across centuries and a quiver of surfboards that get stored in the living room when they aren't on the water, Christopher and Alice have managed to realize a deeply personal, eclectic home. It offers further proof that if you follow your heart, you really can have it all.

**Preceding page:** Surfboards stored in the living room speak to the adventurous nature of the family members.

**Opposite:** Bold art by Eric Yahnker in the foyer contrasts with the house's Federal architectural details.

**Pages 232–33:** The restored original architectural details blend seamlessly with the new, clean-lined built-ins of the living room.

Page 234: A family heirloom painting above a custom banquette in the dining area of the kitchen.

Preceding page: A new wall of glass doors visually connects the kitchen to the garden beyond.

Opposite: In the garden room, a bar with a soapstone sink.

**Above:** A cast-iron soaking tub from Penhaglion in the primary bathroom.

**Opposite:** A walk-in shower with views of the neighborhood.

**Page 240:** Cushy stuffed animals surround an original fireplace in a child's bedroom.

**Page 241:** Art by Iain McKell above an antique bed.

# THE
# BROOKLYN
# REVIVAL

# Brooklyn Heights, Brooklyn — New York

Sometimes, we just can't help ourselves. When we happen to walk by a down-on-its-luck building with a for sale sign out front, our minds begin to wander and we start dreaming about what it could become.

When we saw this 1830s town house in Brooklyn Heights, however, we didn't just dream—we pounced. It turned out that the grand, old building was owned by an order of Catholic nuns who were ready to let it go. It needed plenty of work, because the interior had been cut up into a series of tiny apartments and many of the original window openings had been bricked over; but right away we had a vision for the possibilities.

Because we couldn't actually afford such a building for ourselves, we put together a team to buy it and hatched a plan to renovate and sell it. Then, we completely rebuilt it from the inside out, right down to replacing the floor joists and designing a sweeping new central staircase beneath a skylight. We took off the roof to create a new open-air deck in the former attic, which has views to the East River and Lower Manhattan. And we installed a private planted driveway out back where there was previously just asphalt.

As we dove deeper into the design, we treated the town house as our own. We fell in love with the place, even though we knew we couldn't keep it. We introduced details we had originally conceived for client projects but never used, such as kitchen cabinets with gently curved corners and marble flooring with circular brass inlays. Letting it go at the end of the process was bitter-sweet, but we know there are many other proud old houses just like it waiting for a similar treatment. So, we're always looking for the next one.

**Preceding page:** The town house was completely restored, inside and out.

**Opposite:** The foyer has a floor in Grigio Adriatico marble with brass inlays.

**Pages 246–47:** The generous living room, with a Triad 15 pendant light in blackened brass by Apparatus.

**Page 248:** A detail of the baroque marble mantelpiece, discovered in the basement of the house, that was restored and installed in the living room.

**Preceding page:** A sculptural staircase with a curved steel-and-walnut handrail.

**Opposite:** The radiused-corner upper cabinets frame the La Cornue range in the kitchen.

**Above:** A leather-and-velvet Divine Recline bench from Ochre at the foot of the bed in the primary bedroom.

**Opposite:** A luxurious primary bathroom that welcomes fun in the Balmoral cast-iron bathtub by Cheviot.

## ACKNOWLEDGMENTS

We dedicate this book to our amazing kiddos—Brecken, Harper, Elliott, and Georgia—whom we love deeply and of whom we are so proud. We thank them for their patience and their (mostly) enthusiastic responses to countless trips to construction sites, galleries, furniture fairs, and factories that we seem to take on every vacation. We hope that their exposure to such creative energy and the cultivation of an idea from concept to fruition will lead them to forge their own rewarding paths, each one filled with joy and passion. They are all bright stars, and we can't wait to see what they do.

We would like to each thank our parents for their unconditional love, support, and guidance. They imbued us with problem-solving skills and a passion for innovation, and let us each follow our own paths, even when it wasn't the easiest route for them or us. We thank them for the opportunities we've had to explore, to see great architecture and design, and to learn the value of hard work. We recognize our siblings: Katie and Mike for their strong spirit and perseverance, and Bowie and Jeff for the inspiring creative community that they have fostered. We thank Gabe, Sara, and Finn for being the best partners in Team Brecken. We thank Anela for being the glue that holds our family together. Britt thanks her Aunt Judy for exposing her to such beauty and glamour at a young age. We love you all so much!

We are grateful to Dick Berry and Lucy Commoner for their advice, humor, and guidance. They have shown us that the personal side is most important. We thank John Priber, a true friend and mentor, for teaching us that business can been executed at the highest level and still be fun. We are grateful to Chai Vasarhelyi and Jimmy Chin for partnering with us on multiple creative endeavors and for graciously writing the foreword for this book. We thank Mara Miller and Jesse Carrier for their guidance, for sharing their experiences, and for leading the way. Most importantly, their friendship is everything to us.

Together, we enthusiastically thank all our clients who trusted us with their homes and spaces. They've allowed us to explore and have pushed us to create an expansive breadth of work. We've always said that each project should reflect the client, because we want the result to feel like home. It's an honor to hear their stories, to learn the intricacies and nuances of their lives, and then to design a space that is so personal and hopefully perfect for each of them.

We thank our talented team at Studio DB, both past and present. It goes without saying that it takes a village to create a body of work, and we share this recognition with all of them. Their creativity and hard work continue to elevate our projects, and we are so excited to see what's next. We specifically acknowledge Victor Badami, Julia Bialke, Gabriela Bonilla, Nicole Neil, and Sunny Salkar for their hard work bringing this book to life. One of the most fulfilling parts of our jobs is working with and sourcing from so many immensely gifted product designers, artisans, and fabricators. We've always viewed our work as a collaborative process and cherish the creative partnerships that excite us and expand our imaginations. Most importantly, we have met so many great people and have forged lasting friendships along the way. We thank all of the talented partners who made the magical spaces in this book possible.

It has meant so much that Philip Reeser and Charles Miers at Rizzoli New York believed in us to create this book, and we appreciate their consistent guidance during the process. We still pinch ourselves (not each other) that we have a book published by Rizzoli.

We are so fortunate to have collaborated with Conor Brady. We could not have found a better person to design a book that so perfectly reflects us and our work. Conor made the process so enjoyable, and we thank him for that.

Tim McKeough, the book's writer, has become a trusted friend and collaborator since he wrote about our home nearly a decade ago. We thank him for his enthusiasm, for joining us on this journey, and for capturing the essence of our work so beautifully.

Matthew Williams has so expertly documented our work over the years. It's always invigorating to see our projects through his lens. Additionally, we thank Ian Baguskas, Matt Carbone, and Annie Schlechter for their wonderful photography and for sharing it in this book.

We greatly appreciate the immensely talented stylists Lili Diallo, Hilary Robertson, and Mieke ten Have who each bring a thoughtful and fresh perspective to our work. Their added layers help bring the projects to life.

We thank Ethan Elkins, Nicole Haubner, and the team at Dada Goldberg for the introduction to Rizzoli and for their role in making this publication happen.

Lastly, we want to thank each other. It's not always easy, but it's so rewarding and magical to be able to do it together. We couldn't imagine it any other way.

*Britt and Damian Zunino*

For further information and credits for each project, please scan the QR Code or visit **studiodb.com/drawntogether**

**Page 2:** For the Tudor house project, William Storms created a textile installation, which is draped over an original brass handrail.

**Page 4:** A vintage Camaleonda sectional by Mario Bellini and hand-painted wallpaper by Porter Teleo create a cozy media room.

**Page 254:** A painting by Mel Bochner animates a Greenwich Village living room.

First published in the United States of America in 2025 by
Rizzoli International Publications, Inc.
49 West 27th Street
New York, New York 10001
rizzoliusa.com

**Publisher:** Charles Miers
**Senior Editor:** Philip Reeser
**Production Manager:** Alyn Evans
**Design Coordinator:** Tim Biddick
**Managing Editor:** Lynn Scrabis

**Designer:** Conor Brady

Copyright © 2025 by Studio DB
Text by Britt and Damian Zunino with Tim McKeough
Foreword by Chai Vasarhelyi and Jimmy Chin

All photography by Matthew Williams except images on the following pages:
16 and 181: Ian Baguskas
147, 149, 150–51, 152, 153, and 155: Annie Schlechter
165: Matthew Carbone

ISBN: 978-0-8478-4627-6
Library of Congress Control Number: 2024942686

2025 2026 2027 2028 / 10 9 8 7 6 5 4 3 2 1

Printed in Hong Kong

MIX
Paper | Supporting responsible forestry
FSC™ C023053
FSC
www.fsc.org